CLASSIC
CHRISTIANITY
STUDY
SERIES

A Closer Look at
Law &
Grace

BOB
GEORGE

HARVEST HOUSE PUBLISHERS
Eugene, Oregon 97402

A CLOSER LOOK AT LAW AND GRACE

Copyright © 1993 Harvest House Publishers
Eugene, Oregon 97402

ISBN 1-56507-083-6

Printed in the United States of America.

Contents

No Other
Foundation

As a person's physical growth is based on proper diet and exercise, so is the Christian's spiritual growth dependent on regular feeding upon the Word of God and application of its truth. With more false teaching, shifting opinions, and general confusion in the world than ever before, Christians need a solid foundation upon which to base their beliefs and build their lives. The Word of God declares that Jesus Christ is that foundation of truth. Therefore, the emphasis of the Classic Christianity Study Series is in helping Christians discover for themselves what the Bible actually says about Christ.

These Bible study guides are uniquely prepared for this purpose. They are useful for the newborn, intermediate, or mature Christian in that they begin with the fundamental and central question of who is Jesus Christ and then build upon that foundation in a logical and progressive manner. The Classic Christianity Study Series is also extremely flexible in that it can be used for individual or group study.

The Book of Acts tells us that the first Christians were "continually devoting themselves to the apostles' *teaching* and to *fellowship*, to the *breaking of bread* and to *prayer*" (Acts 2:42). The need for a proper balance in the Christian life is as real today as it was in the first century. The Classic Christianity Study Series has therefore been designed to incorporate all of these elements vital for spiritual growth.

For no man can lay a foundation other than the one
which is laid, which is Jesus Christ (1 Corinthians 3:11).

Helpful Suggestions
as You Begin

1. Choosing a convenient time and location will help you to be consistent in your study.

2. Use a Bible that you are comfortable with.

3. Before beginning your study, always pray and ask God to quiet your heart and open your mind to understand the Scriptures.

4. Approach the Word of God with a learner's heart and a teachable spirit.

1

The Contrast Between Law and Grace

The Word of God makes abundant use of a very helpful teaching tool—contrasts: light and darkness, the kingdom of God and the kingdom of Satan, life and death, lost and saved, just to name a few. And one very beautiful and educational contrast found throughout the Bible is law and grace.

Far from being a dull theological subject, law and grace is the very backbone of the gospel. The difference between the two is at the heart of how a person is saved and, equally important, how a person will live the Christian life. Law and grace is not a side issue, it winds its way into every nook and cranny of the Christian life.

Without a proper understanding of law and grace, a person will be "double minded, and unstable in all his ways" (James 1:8). The Bible will be hopelessly contradictory for such a person and he will be unable to relate to God with confidence and thanksgiving.

However, those who have come to a fuller understanding of the grace under which we live have nearly felt "born again— again." They have regained the joy, freedom, and spontaneity of their earliest Christian experience. This is the truth that sets men free (John 8:32).

Let's take a closer look at law and grace.

Key Verse: John 1:17

For the law was given through Moses; grace and truth came through Jesus Christ.

---

1. What was given through Moses?

2. What came through Jesus Christ?

3. Does this verse imply that there is a difference between what was given through Moses and what came through Jesus Christ?

Some men came down from Judea to Antioch and were teaching the brothers: "Unless you are circumcised, according to the custom taught by Moses, you cannot be saved." . . . Then some of the believers who belonged to the party of the Pharisees stood up and said, "The Gentiles must be circumcised and required to obey the law of Moses" (Acts 15:1,5).

1. According to the men from Judea, what must one do to be saved?

   Circumcision

2. On whose customs did they base their teaching?

   Moses

3. The believers who were Pharisees said that the Gentiles must do two things to be saved. What were they?

   circumcision, obey the law

According to Acts 15:7-11—

1. Who was the first to preach the gospel to the Gentiles?

   Peter

2. How did God show that He accepted the Gentiles?

   Gift of H.S.

3. How were the hearts of the Gentiles cleansed?

   Faith

4. Did God make a distinction between Jew and Gentile concerning His gift of the Holy Spirit and the purifying of hearts?

No

5. What did Peter say the Pharisees were doing by requiring the Gentiles to be circumcised and to observe the law of Moses?

Loading them w/ the burden of Law

6. Is the yoke of the law something that any of us could bear?

No

7. How does Peter conclude that we are saved?

Faith in Jesus

8. Are we saved by the law of Moses or by the grace of Jesus Christ?

J.C.

> So then, just as you received Christ Jesus as Lord, continue to live
> in Him (Colossians 2:6).

1. According to this verse, is there a difference between how we received Christ (were saved) and how we are to live our Christian lives?

No

2. How, then, would you conclude that we are to live our Christian lives—by the law of Moses or by the grace of Jesus Christ?

In 2 Corinthians 3:7-11—

1. How does Paul describe the law?   *Glorious*

2. How does Paul describe the ministry of Jesus Christ?

more Glorious

3. Is there a difference between the two?

Yes

4. How does the glory of the law compare to the glory of that which came through Jesus?

as having no glory

In 2 Corinthians 3:12-18—

1. What did Moses have to do to hide the fact that the radiance of the law was fading away?

hide his face

2. What covers men's hearts when Moses is read today?

minds dull
truth veiled

3. When is this veil taken away?

One turns to Christ

4. When a person turns to the Lord, what will he experience?

Glory from God

5. Whose glory will he reflect?

Christs

6. Into whose likeness will he be transformed?

Same

7. Could a person reflect the glory of the Lord, experience freedom, and be transformed into the likeness of the Lord through what was given by Moses—the law?

No

8. Who is the source of these things?

God

He has made us competent as ministers of a new covenant—not of the letter but of the Spirit; for the letter kills, but the Spirit gives life (2 Corinthians 3:6).

1. God made Paul a competent minister of what?

    Grace   New Covenant

2. Is this new covenant of the letter or of the Spirit?

3. What does the letter do?

    Kills, destroys

4. What does the Spirit do?

    Life

5. Why do you think it is important to know the difference between law and grace?

    To live letter of law kills the human spirit because of continual failure & guilt. To live by Grace sets/frees our spirits free to serve him w/ joy because of forgiveness, Adoption, election, redemption & H.S. in our ♡'s

2

A Closer Look at the Law

The passages of Scripture we studied in Chapter 1 narrowed the definition of *law* to what was given to Moses and *grace* to what came through Jesus Christ. This is not to say that law did not exist before Moses, or that grace did not exist before Jesus. For example, law can be seen in the Garden of Eden when God said to Adam, "Do not eat of the tree of the knowledge of good and evil" (Genesis 2:17). Likewise, grace can be seen when God killed an innocent animal to provide clothing for Adam and Eve after the fall (Genesis 3:21). Law and grace have always existed, but "the law" and "the grace" refer specifically to Moses and to the work of Jesus Christ, respectively.

The law consists of the Ten Commandments and the ceremonial laws given to Moses at Mount Sinai. Israel had lived in bondage to the Egyptians for 430 years. By His miraculous power, God split the Red Sea and Moses led the people across on dry land. When the Egyptians tried to follow, the sea returned to normal and all of Pharoah's army drowned. Israel was free. The Israelites traveled from place to place, and after three months set up camp at the foot of Mount Sinai. There, God met with Moses and established the law for the nation of Israel.

As we saw in Chapter 1, the grace of Jesus Christ was and is far superior to the law that was given at Mount Sinai. So why was the law given? What role did it play for the Israelites, and what role does it play in our lives? With these questions in mind, let's take a closer look at the law.

Key Verse: Exodus 19:3-5

Then Moses went up to God, and the LORD called to him from the mountain and said, "This is what you are to say to the house of Jacob and what you are to tell the people of Israel: 'You yourselves have seen what I did to Egypt, and how I carried you on eagles' wings and brought you to myself. Now if you obey me fully and keep my covenant, then out of all nations you will be my treasured possession.' "

------

1. Who met with God on the mountain?

   Mose

2. To whom did God ask Moses to speak?

   People of Israel

3. Who, then, was the law for?

   Jews

4. What had God done for the Israelites?

   Rescued them from bondage

5. In light of these things, God makes a proposal to the nation. What two things did He require of them?

   obey me fully
   Keep my covenant

6. What would be the results of fulfilling these requirements?

   your My possesion

Moses then wrote down everything the LORD had said. He got up early the next morning and built an altar at the foot of the mountain and set up twelve stone pillars representing the twelve tribes of Israel. Then he sent young Israelite men, and they offered burnt offerings and sacrificed young bulls as fellowship offerings to the LORD. Moses took half of the blood and put it in bowls, and the other half he sprinkled on the altar. Then he took the Book of the Covenant and read it to the people. They responded, "We will do everything the LORD has said; we will obey." Moses then took the blood, sprinkled it on the people and said, "This is the blood of the covenant that the LORD has made with you in accordance with all these words" (Exodus 24:4-8).

1. What did Moses write down?

Commandment

2. What did he read to the people?

Book of Covenant

3. What was their response?

Position to obey

4. How did Moses inaugurate this covenant?

sprinkle w/ sacrificial blood

5. Who was this covenant between?

Israel & God

6. Are we a part of this covenant that God made between Himself and the nation of Israel?

No

According to Deuteronomy 6:20-25—

1. Why did God bring the Israelites out of Egypt?

2. Did God ever promise to give you a land like He promised the Israelites?

3. Were you ever a slave of Pharoah in Egypt?

4. Romans 7:14 reads, "We know that the law is spiritual; but I am unspiritual, sold as a slave to sin." Even though we were not slaves to Pharoah, what does this say we were slaves to?   *Sin*

5. Why did the Lord command the Israelites to obey all the decrees that He gave to Moses on Mount Sinai?   *to be my people on Moses*

6. If the nation of Israel was careful to obey all the commandments, what would their obedience be for them?   *Salvation Righteousness*

7. Romans 3:20 reads, "Therefore no one will be declared righteous in his sight by observing the law; rather, through the law we become conscious of sin." According to this verse, can an individual gain righteousness through obedience to the law?   *No*

8. The promise of a new land and righteousness as spoken of in Deuteronomy were directed toward whom?   *Jew*

> *If you fully obey the LORD your God and carefully follow all his commands I give you today, the LORD your God will set you high above all the nations on earth. All these blessings will come upon you and accompany you if you obey the LORD your God* (Deuteronomy 28:1,2).

1. What did Israel have to do to be set high above all the nations on earth?   *fully obey & follow commands*

2. How were they to obey the Lord, and how many of His commands were they to follow?   *fully, all*

3. What else did God say would happen to Israel if they obeyed?   *blessed*

4. Read through the blessings of God listed in Deutoronomy 28:2-14. Are these blessings spiritual or physical in nature? *but affect them spiritually*

> *However, if you do not obey the LORD your God and do not carefully follow all his commands and decrees I am giving you today, all these curses will come upon you and overtake you* (Deuteronomy 28:15).

1. What would happen to Israel if they did not obey the commands of God?

Curse

2. Read through the curses listed in Deuteronomy 28. Are these curses physical or spiritual in nature?

but certainty affecting them spiritually

> *What, then, was the purpose of the law? It was added because of transgressions until the Seed to whom the promise referred had come* (Galatians 3:19).

1. How long was the law to last for the nation of Israel?

until the Messiah

2. Who do you think the Seed refers to in this verse?

Jesus

3. Since the law was only to last until the Seed had come, do you think God had something better for Israel than the law?

yes

4. Do you think God has something better for us?

yes

God oftentimes uses physical pictures to communicate spiritual truth. For example, Jesus pointed to the relationship between a vine and branch to show us what our relationship to Him is like. God uses the law in much the same way. As we will see, the law is spiritual in nature and has a spiritual purpose in our lives. What was given to Moses and the nation of Israel is a physical picture to help us understand just what the spiritual purpose of the law is.

> *So then, the law is holy, and the commandment is holy, righteous and good. . . . We know that the law is spiritual; but I am unspiritual, sold as a slave to sin* (Romans 7:12,14).

1. How does Paul describe the law?   Holy, righteous, good

2. Is the law spiritual or physical in nature?

3. Since we are not part of the nation of Israel and, therefore, not included in the covenant that God made with Israel, would the law have a different purpose in our lives than it did for the nation of Israel?

No

4. Since Paul described the law as spiritual in nature, would it be correct to conclude that the law has a spiritual purpose in our lives?

Yes

The covenant that God established at Mount Sinai was between Himself and the nation of Israel. The laws He gave were for the good of the nation of Israel, so they could prosper and live. If they obeyed the law, they would receive physical blessings. If they disobeyed, they would receive physical curses. The Old Testament records the history of Israel, the blessings and curses they received as a result of their obedience and disobedience. It is fascinating to read and encouraging to see God's faithfulness to Israel.

But God has something much better for you and me. It is a spiritual blessing received through the person of Jesus Christ. The law has a spiritual purpose in our lives, and we will discuss this purpose in our next lesson.

3

The Purpose
of the Law

As we learned in the last chapter, the law was given to the nation of Israel and the specific blessings and curses applied to them. We also learned that the law has a separate and spiritual purpose. That purpose is found in answer to the question, "Who turns to Christ for salvation?" Only those who know they need to be saved. And that is the purpose of the law, to point out our need for salvation.

Key Verse: Galatians 3:19

What, then, was the purpose of the law? It was added because of transgressions until the Seed to whom the promise referred had come.

1. What was Paul's question concerning the law?

   teacher, Schoolmaster Authority Instruc

2. Have you ever asked this question concerning the law?

   Yes

3. According to this verse, why was the law added?

   to show us our sin

4. How long was the law to remain in effect?   *until the seed*

5. Galatians 3:16 reads, "The promises were spoken to Abraham and to his seed. The Scripture does not say 'and to seeds,' meaning many people, but 'and to your seed,' meaning one person, who is Christ." According to this verse, who is the seed?

> *The law was added so that the trespass might increase. But where sin increased, grace increased all the more, so that, just as sin reigned in death, so also grace might reign through righteousness to bring eternal life through Jesus Christ our Lord* (Romans 5:20,21).

1. According to this verse, why was the law added?

   We become aware of sin

2. This seems odd that God would want sin to increase, but the verse goes on to tell us why. Where sin increased, what else increased all the more?

   Grace

3. Why did God want grace to increase all the more?

   Like the sinful woman who saw her sad state first & then saw the forgiving savior

4. When grace reigns through righteousness, what does it bring?

   Eternal life & peace

5. Who does this eternal life come through?

   Jesus

6. So why do you think God gave the law?

   Stepping stone to Messiah

> *We know that the law is good if one uses it properly. We also know that law is made not for the righteous but for lawbreakers and rebels, the ungodly and sinful, the unholy and irreligious; for those who kill*

*their fathers or mothers, for murderers, for adulterers and perverts, for
slave traders and liars and perjurers—and for whatever else is contrary
to the sound doctrine* (1 Timothy 1:8-10).

1. What does this passage say about the law when it is used properly?

   law is good

2. Is the law made for the righteous?

   no

3. Who are the righteous? Are they lost or saved?

   Saved

4. Who is the law made for?

   sinner

5. What would you conclude, then, concerning the law? Is it for the lost or the
saved?

   lost

*Now we know that whatever the law says, it says to those who are
under the law, so that every mouth may be silenced and the whole world
held accountable to God. Therefore no one will be declared righteous in
his sight by observing the law; rather, through the law we become
conscious of sin* (Romans 3:19,20).

1. To whom does the law speak?

   those under law

2. Who is under the law?

   World for Jew & Proselytes

3. According to this passage, what does the law say to those under the law?

   guilty

4. How many people will be declared righteous in God's sight by observing the law?

None

5. What do we become conscious of through the law?

Sin

6. Why would you need to become conscious of sin?

to see a need for a savior from sin

> . . . *because law brings wrath. And where there is no law there is no transgression* (Romans 4:15).

1. Is there transgression (sin) where there is no law?

yes

2. Then, what does the law do in our lives?

spotlite sin

3. According to this verse, what does the law bring about?

wrath judgment

4. Since the law brings wrath, can you separate the punishment of the law from the law?

no

> *Therefore, just as sin entered the world through one man, and death through sin, and in this way death came to all men, because all sinned—for before the law was given, sin was in the world. But sin is not taken into account when there is no law* (Romans 5:12,13).

1. How did sin enter the world?

Adam & Eve

2. Who was this one man?

Adam

3. What else entered the world as a result of Adam's sin?

Death

4. Death spread to how many men? For what reason?

All because all sin

5. Was sin in the world before the law was given?

yes

6. But when is sin taken into account?

?

7. So, did the law bring about sin in our lives, or did the law merely point out the sin that was already there as a result of Adam's sin?

later

> *What shall we say, then? Is the law sin? Certainly not! Indeed I would not have known what sin was except through the law. For I would not have known what coveting really was if the law had not said, "Do not covet." But sin, seizing the opportunity afforded by the commandment, produced in me every kind of covetous desire. For apart from law, sin is dead. Once I was alive apart from law; but when the commandment came, sin sprang to life and I died. I found that the very commandment that was intended to bring life actually brought death. For sin, seizing the opportunity afforded by the commandment, deceived me, and through the commandment put me to death. So then, the law is holy, and the commandment is holy, righteous and good. Did that which is good, then, become death to me? By no means! But in order that sin might be recognized as sin, it produced death in me through what was good, so that through the commandment sin might become utterly sinful* (Romans 7:7-13).

1. From the passages of Scripture we have looked at so far, we might conclude that the law brought sin into the world. In anticipation of this conclusion, what question did Paul ask and answer in these verses?

Is the law sin

2. How did Paul find out what sin was?

law defined his desires as evil

3. If the law had not said, "Do not covet," would Paul have known he was coveting?

No

4. Would we know about our sin apart from the law? *or a law*

No

5. What did sin do in Paul's life through the opportunity afforded by the commandment?

6. What does sin do in our lives through the opportunity afforded by the commandment?

7. Does this mean that the law produced the sin, or that the law merely *shows* us the sin in our lives?

8. How does Paul describe sin apart from the law?

dead

9. What happened to Paul when the commandment came?

Sin was realized

10. What did the commandment bring? (Contrast this to what grace brings in Romans 5:20,21: "The law was added so that the trespass might increase. But where sin increased, grace increased all the more, so that, just as sin reigned in death, so also grace might reign through righteousness to bring eternal life through Jesus Christ our Lord.")

11. How does Paul describe the law?

12. What did Paul think about the law's action in his life (showing him his sin and his state of death)? Was it good or bad?

13. Is God's purpose for the law in your life good or bad?

14. Through the commandment, what does sin become?

15. Has sin become utterly sinful in your life and have you recognized it for what it truly is? If not, are you willing to let the law do its work in your life?

> But the Scripture declares that the whole world is a prisoner of sin, so that what was promised, being given through faith in Jesus Christ, might be given to those who believe. Before this faith came, we were held prisoners by the law, locked up until faith should be revealed. So the law was put in charge to lead us to Christ that we might be justified by faith (Galalatians 3:22-24).

1. What does the Scripture declare concerning the whole world?

2. How is the promise given?

3. Who is able to receive the promise?

4. What held us prisoners to our sin?

5. For how long was the law to keep us locked up?

6. Why was the law put in charge?

7. Why was the law put in charge to lead us to Christ?

8. Apart from the law, would you ever know that you were lost and in need of salvation?

4

What the Law
Is Powerless to Do

As we saw in the last chapter, the law is like a mirror. It can show us that our faces are dirty, but it can't wash them for us. And that is all God intended the law to do. It shows us that we are dead in our sins and in need of life, but it is powerless to do anything else.

Key Verse: Hebrews 7:18,19

The former regulation is set aside because it was weak and useless (for the law made nothing perfect), and a better hope is introduced, by which we draw near to God.

1. According to the writer of Hebrews, what has happened to the law (former regulation)?

2. Why was the law set aside?

3. Why does he say that the law is weak and useless?

4. Because the law makes nothing perfect, can it allow us to draw near to God?

5. According to this verse, what do we need to draw near to God?

6. Would the grace of God provide that better hope?

> *The law is only a shadow of the good things that are coming—not the realities themselves. For this reason it can never, by the same sacrifices repeated endlessly year after year, make perfect those who draw near to worship* (Hebrews 10:1).

1. How does the writer of Hebrews describe the law?

2. How much power does a shadow have?

3. Because the law is a shadow, can you depend on it to make you right with God?

4. Can the law make you perfect and enable you to draw near to God?

> *For what the law was powerless to do in that it was weakened by the flesh, God did by sending his own Son in the likeness of sinful man to be a sin offering* (Romans 8:3).

1. How does Paul describe the law in this verse?

2. What made the law powerless?

3. Is the problem the law, or is the problem you and me?

4. Do we have the power to save ourselves?

5. Who does?

The Law Cannot Make Us Righteous

I do not set aside the grace of God, for if righteousness could be gained through the law, Christ died for nothing! (Galatians 2:21).

1. Does the law have the ability to make us righteous?

2. If it did, what would we have to conclude about Christ's death on the cross?

3. What would we have to do with the grace of God if obedience to the law could make us righteous?

4. Would the grace of God have any value in our lives if righteousness could be gained through the law?

Clearly no one is justified before God by the law, because, "The righteous will live by faith" (Galatians 3:11).

1. Can anyone be justified or declared totally righteous in the sight of God by the law?

2. How do the righteous live?

3. Does the law have the power to make us righteous?

> *Know that a man is not justified by observing the law, but by faith in Jesus Christ. So we, too, have put our faith in Christ Jesus that we may be justified by faith in Christ and not by observing the law, because by observing the law no one will be justified* (Galatians 2:16).

1. Can a man be justified by observing the law?

2. How is a person justified?

3. What did Paul say that he did to be justified?

4. Should we depend on the law to be justified, or should we put our faith in Christ as Paul did?

The Law Cannot Give Life

> *Is the law, therefore, opposed to the promises of God? Absolutely not! For if a law had been given that could impart life, then righteousness would certainly have come by the law* (Galatians 3:21).

1. Is the law opposed to the promises of God?

2. However, does the law have the ability to impart or give life?

3. If it did, how would righteousness come to you and me?

> *I found that the very commandment that was intended to bring life actually brought death* (Romans 7:10).

1. What did Paul think the commandment (the law) had the power to give him?

2. What did the commandment actually bring to Paul?

3. Does the law have the ability to give life to you and me?

4. What does the law bring?

> *But because of his great love for us, God, who is rich in mercy, made us alive with Christ even when we were dead in transgressions—it is by grace you have been saved* (Ephesians 2:4,5).

1. Who made us alive with Christ?

2. What motivated God to do so?

3. How does this verse say that we are saved?

4. For you and me to receive life and then experience life, what must we depend on—the law or the grace of God?

5. In your own life, what are you depending on for your righteousness and life—your obedience to the law or the grace of God?

6. If you are depending on your obedience to the law, are you willing to recognize that the law is powerless to produce these things in your life?

7. The writer of Hebrews stated that the former regulation was set aside because it was weak and useless. Are you willing to set aside the law in your own life and totally depend on the grace of God?

5

Christ Fulfilled the Law

___

We concluded the previous chapter with the question, "Are you willing to set aside the law in your life and totally depend on the grace of God?" We asked this question based on the fact that the law is powerless to do anything in your life except to point out your sinfulness. It cannot make you righteous or give you eternal life.

There is another reason, however, to set aside the law: Every requirement of the law has been fulfilled through Jesus Christ.

___

Key Verse: Matthew 5:17,18

Do not think that I have come to abolish the law and the prophets; I have not come to abolish them but to fulfill them.

___

1. Did Christ come to abolish the law and the prophets?

2. What did Christ come to do concerning the Law or the Prophets?

3. Who did Jesus say would fulfill the law?

4. In John 5:39, Jesus says, "You diligently study the Scriptures because you think that by them you possess eternal life. These are the Scriptures that testify about me." What Scriptures testify about Jesus?

5. In light of this, how much sense would it make for Jesus to abolish something that is about Him?

> *He said to them, "This is what I told you while I was still with you: Everything must be fulfilled that is written about me in the Law of Moses, the Prophets and the Psalms"* (Luke 24:44).

1. What did Jesus tell the disciples while He was still with them?

2. How much written about Jesus did He say must be fulfilled?

3. Do you think Jesus has the ability to fulfill the law?

4. What about us? Do we have the ability to fulfill the law?

Jesus Lived a Sinless Life

> *For we do not have a high priest who is unable to sympathize with our weaknesses, but we have one who was tempted in every way, just as we are—yet was without sin* (Hebrews 4:15).

1. How is Christ referred to in this verse?

2. As our high priest, is Christ able to sympathize with our weaknesses?

3. What is the reason He is able to sympathize with our weaknesses?

4. Even though He was tempted as we are, did Jesus ever sin?

5. Therefore did Jesus ever break one of the commandments God gave to Moses?

Jesus Walked in Perfect Love

As the Father has loved me, so have I loved you. Now remain in my love (John 15:9).

1. How did Jesus say that He loved you and me?

2. How do you think the Father loved Jesus?

3. How would you conclude that Jesus loved you and me?

Love does no harm to its neighbor. Therefore love is the fulfillment of the law (Romans 13:10).

1. According to this verse, does love do any harm to its neighbor?

2. What is the fulfillment of the law?

3. Did Jesus fulfill the law in loving you and me as the Father loved Him?

> *Greater love has no one than this, that he lay down his life for his friends* (John 15:13).

1. What is the greatest love a person could have for another?

2. What was Christ's ultimate act of love toward you and me?

3. If love is the fulfillment of the law, then, ultimately, how did Christ fulfill the law?

Christ Paid the Penalty for Our Sins

> *For the wages of sin is death, but the gift of God is eternal life in Christ Jesus our Lord* (Romans 6:23).

1. Under the law, what is the wages of sin?

2. In contrast, what is the gift of God?

3. What had to be paid before God could give us eternal life?

4. Who paid the wages for our sin?

> *He is the one who turns aside God's wrath, taking away our sins,*
> *and not only ours but also the sins of the whole world* (1 John 2:2).

1. Who turned aside God's wrath on our behalf?

2. What did He do with our sins?

3. What about the sins of the whole world?

4. Did Christ's death on the cross fulfill the law which said, "The wages of sin is death"?

5. For whom did He fulfill the law?

> *He forgave us all our sins, having canceled the written code, with*
> *its regulation, that was against us and that stood opposed to us; he took*
> *it away, nailing it to the cross* (Colossians 2:13,14).

1. How many of our sins did Christ forgive?

2. Since Christ forgave all our sins, what can we conclude about His death on the cross paying for the wages of sin?

3. What did Christ do with the written code?

4. Once he canceled the law, what did Jesus do with it?

5. Therefore, where should the law remain?

> *For what the law was powerless to do in that it was weakened by the flesh, God did by sending his own Son in the likeness of sinful man to be a sin offering. And so he condemned sin in sinful man, in order that the righteous requirements of the law might be fully met in us, who do not live according to the flesh but according to the Spirit* (Romans 8:3,4).

1. What was the law powerless to do?

2. What was the law weakened by?

3. Jesus came to this earth in the likeness of sinful man to be what?

4. As a sin offering, what did He condemn?

5. Why did Jesus condemn sin in sinful man?

6. So, have the righteous requirements of the law been fully met in us?

7. Who fulfilled them?

8. If Christ has fulfilled the entire law, does it make sense for us to try to fulfill the law through our self-efforts?

Jesus did not come to abolish the law, He came to fulfill it. Every requirement the law demanded, Jesus fulfilled. He lived a sinless life; He walked in perfect love; and His death on the cross paid in full the wages of sin for the entire world. Christ did it all.

God knew that you and I could never fulfill the law. In fact, He never expected us to. However, when we trust the only One who could fulfill the law, the righteous requirements of the law are met in us. We can set aside the law because it has been fulfilled, canceled, and taken away. God nailed it to the cross, and that is where it is to stay.

6

Christ Redeemed Us from the Law

Redeem is a word that most of us are familiar with. It's what we used to do with green stamps. We'd exchange them for a toaster or something else of value at a redemption center. The biblical definition of redeem is bigger than this green stamp illustration.

The complete meaning of *redeem* is to buy back *and* set free. As we take a closer look at redemption, we will see this is exactly what Jesus Christ has done for you and me through His death on the cross.

Key Verse: Galatians 3:13,14

Christ redeemed us from the curse of the law by becoming a curse for us, for it is written: "Cursed is everyone who is hung on a tree." He redeemed us in order that the blessing given to Abraham might come to the Gentiles through Christ Jesus, so that by faith we might receive the promise of the Spirit.

---

1. What did Christ redeem us from?

2. How did He redeem us?

3. How did Christ become a curse for us?

4. For what reason did Christ redeem us?

5. Who does the blessing given to Abraham come through?

6. When we put our faith in Jesus Christ, what do we receive?

7. Could we receive the promised Holy Spirit if Christ had not redeemed us from the law?

The biblical definition of redemption can best be explained by using the analogy of a slave market. In Jesus' day, the slave market was an integral part of society, a gathering place where slaves were bought and sold. A slave was placed on the auction blocks and could be purchased for a price. Once purchased, the slave became the property of his new owner.

Jesus Christ paid a price to purchase us out of the slave market. He purchased us, however, not to make us slaves again, but to set us free from the law of sin and death.

> *No man can redeem the life of another or give to God a ransom for him—the ransom for a life is costly, no payment is ever enough* (Psalm 49:7,8).

1. According to this verse, could we redeem the life of another?

2. Could we give to God a ransom for the life of another? Why not?

3. Would any payment we offered to God ever be enough?

4. Who, therefore, is the only One who could redeem us?

> *For you know that it was not with perishable things such as silver or gold that you were redeemed from the empty way of life handed down to you from your forefathers, but with the precious blood of Christ, a lamb without blemish or defect* (1 Peter 1:18,19).

1. According to this passage, were silver and gold enough to redeem us?

No

2. What price had to be paid? *Blood of JC*

3. How does Peter describe Jesus Christ? *Perfect Lamb*

4. How does Peter describe the life we were redeemed from?

Empty

5. Before you knew Christ, how would you describe your life?

Aimless Insecure

6. Could any other price except the blood of Jesus purchase us?

> *"Then you will know the truth, and the truth will set you free." They answered him, "We are Abraham's descendants and have never been slaves of anyone. How can you say that we shall be set free?" Jesus replied, "I tell you the truth, everyone who sins is a slave to sin"* (John 8:32-34).

1. How did the Pharisees respond to Jesus' proclamation that the truth would set them free?

2. What did Jesus say they were slaves to?

3. Therefore, what will truth set us free from?

> *But the Scripture declares that the whole world is a prisoner of sin, so that what was promised, being given through faith in Jesus Christ, might be given to those who believe. Before this faith came, we were held prisoners by the law, locked up until faith should be revealed* (Galatians 3:22,23).

1. What is the whole world a prisoner of?

2. What held us prisoners to sin?

3. Since it was the law that held us prisoners to our sin, what is it, then, that demands payment for our release from sin?

4. What payment does the law demand?

5. Has the price been paid to release us from our bondage to sin?

> *He did not enter by means of the blood of goats and calves; but he entered the Most Holy Place once for all by his own blood, having obtained eternal redemption. . . . For this reason Christ is the mediator of a new covenant, that those who are called may receive the promised eternal inheritance—now that he has died as a ransom to set them free from the sins committed under the first covenant* (Hebrews 9:12,15).

1. What did Christ obtain when He entered the Most Holy Place?

2. How did He enter the Most Holy Place?

3. What, then, was the price for our eternal redemption?

4. Was the blood of bulls and goats enough?

5. What is Christ the mediator of?

6. Under this new covenant, what do those who are called receive?

7. How does the writer of Hebrews describe Christ's death on the cross?

8. What did Christ's ransom set us free from?

9. Could we be under a new covenant and receive the promised eternal inheritance without first being set free from the sins committed under the old covenant?

10. How important, then, is it, for us to know we have been redeemed from the law?

> *Therefore, there is now no condemnation for those who are in Christ Jesus, because through Christ Jesus the law of the Spirit of life set me free from the law of sin and death* (Romans 8:1,2).

1. Is there any condemnation for those who are in Christ?

2. Why is there no condemnation for those who are in Christ?

3. What has the Spirit of life set us free from?

4. Based on the verses we have looked at in this chapter, what sets us free from the law of sin and death?

> *But when the time had fully come, God sent his Son, born of a woman, born under law, to redeem those under law, that we might receive the full rights of sons. Because you are sons, God sent the Spirit of his Son into our hearts, the Spirit who calls out, "Abba, Father." So you are no longer a slave, but a son; and since you are a son, God has made you also an heir* (Galatians 4:4-7).

1. Why did God send His Son?

2. For what reason did God redeem us?

3. Did God buy us out of the slave market to keep us as slaves or to make us sons?

4. What did God do to assure us we are sons?

5. What does the Spirit call out?

6. Because we are sons, can we ever be slaves again?

7. Because God paid the price through the death of His Son, to whom do we belong?

8. Because we are sons, what else have we become?

> *It is for freedom that Christ has set us free. Stand firm, then, and do not let yourselves be burdened again by a yoke of slavery* (Galatians 5:1).

1. Why did Christ set us free from the law of sin and death?

2. What is the yoke of slavery that could burden us again?

3. Once we have been purchased by God and set free from the law of sin and death, does God ever want us to go back to the law?

> *In Him we have redemption through his blood, the forgiveness of sins, in accordance with the riches of God's grace that He lavished on us with all wisdom and understanding* (Ephesians 1:7,8).

1. What do we have if we are in Christ?

2. Once again, how was our redemption obtained?

3. What is our redemption in Christ in accordance with?

You and I were born into this world as slaves to sin. We were held captive to our sinfulness by the law. For us to be set free, a price had to be paid. The price the law demanded was the precious blood of Jesus Christ. Nothing else would do.

At the right time God sent Jesus Christ into the world to pay the price the law demanded. He redeemed us from the law of sin and death. He did so not to keep us as slaves, but to set us free, to make us His sons, and to give us the full rights of heirs. This is our redemption.

The Bible tells us to stand firm, therefore, in the freedom that we have as sons of God. It just doesn't make sense to go back to the law, back to what kept us in slavery.

7

No Longer
Under the Law

The purpose of the law is to show us our need for salvation and then point us to Christ. Once it has done this, the law serves no other purpose. It cannot save us, give us life, forgive our sins, or make us righteous. That is why, as believers, we are no longer under the law; we are under the grace of God.

Key Verse: Galatians 3:24,25

So the law was put in charge to lead us to Christ that we might be justified by faith. Now that faith has come, we are no longer under the supervision of the law.

1. According to this verse, why was the law put in charge?

    Show us our need

2. When we are led to Christ, how are we justified?

    His blood

3. Now that faith has come, are we under the supervision of the law any longer?

    No

4. If the law has led you to Christ so you could be justified by faith in Him, has the law served its purpose in your life?

Yes

5. Since the law has served its purpose, is there any further need for the law in your life?

No

> *Do you not know, brothers—for I am speaking to men who know the law—that the law has authority over a man only as long as he lives? For example, by law a married woman is bound to her husband as long as he is alive, but if her husband dies, she is released from the law of marriage. So then, if she marries another man while her husband is still alive, she is called an adulteress. But if her husband dies, she is released from that law and is not an adulteress, even though she marries another man* (Romans 7:1-3)

1. How long does the law have authority over a person?

Only the Living

2. To explain his point, Paul uses the example of marriage. How long is a woman bound to her husband?

life

3. What happens if her husband dies?

she's free from the marriage

4. What does the law call the woman who marries another man while her husband is still alive?

Adulterer

5. If her husband dies and she marries another man, is she an adulteress? Why not?

A) No B) she's free from law

> *So, my brothers, you also died to the law through the body of Christ, that you might belong to another, to him who was raised from the dead, in order that we might bear fruit to God. For when we were*

controlled by the sinful nature, the sinful passions aroused by the law were at work in our bodies, so that we bore fruit for death. But now, by dying to what once bound us, we have been released from the law so that we serve in the new way of the Spirit, and not in the old way of the written code (Romans 7:4-6).

1. According to this passage, what have we died to? *Law*

2. How did we die to the law? *Through Christ*

3. Now that we have died to the law, are we free to belong to another?

   Yes

4. To whom do we now belong? *JC.*

5. Now that we belong to Christ, what kind of fruit do we bear?

   fruit of Spirit Gal 5:22-3

6. Could we bear fruit to God under the law?

   No

7. What kind of fruit did we bear while under the law?

   Sinful

8. What did the law do to our sinful passions?

   aroused awakened

9. Because we have died to what once bound us, what have we been released from?

   sinful nature

10. How do we now serve? *of the Spirit*

11. Before we were released from the law, how did we serve?

Law bound us to sin

12. Could we serve in the new way of the Spirit while under the law?

No

13. How important, then, is it to realize that we are no longer under the authority of the law?

Exstremely

> *For sin shall not be your master, because you are not under law, but under grace* (Romans 6:14).

1. According to this verse, what is the reason that sin shall not be your master?

because we're under grace

2. As believers, what are we now under?

Grace

3. Therefore, what is to control our lives—law or grace?

4. Who is full of grace? *J.C. John 1*
hopefully us

5. Because we are under grace, who are we controlled by?

H.S.

6. Could we be controlled by Jesus Christ under the law?

No ? Maybe soverngly

Scripture spells it out clearly: The law has no place in a believer's life. We are under the grace of God.

But many people try to mix law and grace in their Christian life. They claim to be saved by the grace of God but then they feel they must do something to make themselves acceptable to God. For those who may think the law does play a role in the believer's life, let's take a closer look at what it means to live under the law.

8

Hopelessness Under the Law

In the simplest of terms, law and grace is the issue of God's acceptance. On what basis is a person made acceptable to God? There are only three possible answers. According to the law, man is responsible to make himself acceptable to God through obedience to the law. According to grace, God gives man a standing of total acceptance as a gift through His Son, Jesus Christ. And finally, in an attempt to mix law and grace, man says that God's grace enables him to work for his acceptance. Whatever answer we choose affects not only how we approach the Christian life, but our very understanding of God's love as well.

Many of us believe that we are made acceptable by the grace of God, yet we experience fear, guilt, and condemnation. That indicates we have not let go of the law. For some reason, we still think we can make ourselves acceptable to God, so we persist in bringing the law into our Christian life. In order to let go of the law, we need to understand its stringency. With that in mind, let's take a closer look at life under the law.

The Law's Standard Is Perfection

Key Verse: James 2:10

For whoever keeps the whole law and yet stumbles at just one point is guilty of breaking all of it.

1. How much of the law must be broken in order to be guilty of breaking all of it?

2. How much of the law must be kept in order to obey it?

all

3. Will anything less than 100 percent obedience do when it comes to the law?

no

4. Since the law's standard is perfection, does it offer any hope to those trying to live up to the law? Why or why not?   *No   Impossibly*

5. What kinds of feelings will failure to keep the entire law produce in a person's life?   *guilt   condemnation*

> Be perfect, therefore, as your heavenly Father is perfect (Matthew 5:48).

1. In this verse, who does Jesus say we should measure ourselves against?

God Father

2. How perfect is our heavenly Father?   *Perfectly Perfect*

3. According to this standard, how many of us measure up?

— 0 —

4. If you are trying to gain God's acceptance through keeping the law and the law's standard is perfection, what would you probably conclude about your acceptance before God?   *M.I.*

5. What would you conclude about the love of God?

Don't Love me

All who rely on observing the law are under a curse, for it is written: "Cursed is everyone who does not continue to do everything written in the Book of the Law" (Galatians 3:10).

1. According to this verse, what is a person under who relies on observing the law? *cursed*

2. To avoid being under a curse, how much of the law does a person have to do? *all*

3. Is it possible to continue doing everything written in the book of the law every minute of every day for your entire life? *no*

4. So, how much hope does the law offer to those who try to live up to it?

- 0 -

5. Based on this verse, what is the only thing a person can expect from the law? *continual cursing, condemnation*

6. Since condemnation and guilt are what people experience through trying to keep the law to gain God's acceptance, what would they likely conclude about God's love for them? *Angry old man*

The Law Amplified by Christ

You have heard that it was said, "Do not commit adultery." But I tell you that anyone who looks at a woman lustfully has already committed adultery with her in his heart. If your right eye causes you to sin, gouge it out and throw it away. It is better for you to lose one part of your body than for your whole body to be thrown into hell (Matthew 5:27-29).

1. In this passage, what does the law say concerning adultery?

Do not do it

2. How does Jesus define adultery?   *Look on another w/ lust*

3. Where does Jesus say the act of adultery begins?   *in the mind*

4. Does Jesus make a distinction between outward obedience and the attitude of the heart?   *Yes*

5. What did Jesus say we should do if our eye causes us to sin?   *pluck it out*

6. If we actually did gouge out our eyes, how many of us would be able to read and answer this question?   *few if any*

> You have heard that it was said to the people long ago, "Do not murder, and anyone who murders will be subject to judgment." But I tell you that anyone who is angry with his brother will be subject to judgment. Again, anyone who says to his brother, "Raca," is answerable to the Sanhedrin. But anyone who says, "You fool!" will be in danger of the fire of hell (Matthew 5:21-22).

1. What does the law say about murder?   *subject to judgment*

2. If anyone does murder, what will they be subject to?   *''*

3. According to Jesus, what does it take for a person to be subject to judgment?   *to be angry w/ bro*

4. What do you think Jesus is saying about murder and being angry at your brother?   *Same attitude*

5. Have you ever been angry at someone? According to this passage, what are you guilty of? *Murder*

6. Jesus also says in these verses that anyone who calls another a "fool" is in danger of the fire of hell. How difficult is it to keep the law under these conditions? *Difficult   What about Paul Killing Christians?*

7. After looking at these verses, would you say there is any hope for living a perfect life under the law? *No*

> *Woe to you, teachers of the law and Pharisees, you hypocrites! You clean the outside of the cup and dish, but inside they are full of greed and self-indulgence* (Matthew 23:25).

1. What does Jesus call the teachers of the law and the Pharisees?
hypocrites

2. Why does He call them hypocrites? *they focus on outward*

3. On the outside they appear clean, but on the inside they are full of what?
greed & self indulgence

> *Woe to you, teachers of the law and Pharisees, you hypocrites! You are like whitewashed tombs, which look beautiful on the outside but on the inside are full of dead men's bones and everything unclean. In the same way, on the outside you appear to people as righteous but on the inside you are full of hypocrisy and wickedness* (Matthew 23:27,28).

1. Once again, Jesus calls the teachers of the law and the Pharisees hypocrites. What does He compare them to in this passage? *whitewashed tombs*

2. What is a whitewashed tomb like on the outside?

   beautiful

3. What are the tombs full of on the inside?

   stink

4. How did the teachers of the law and the Pharisees appear to people on the outside?

   pietis

5. What did Jesus say they were full of on the inside?

   dead bones

6. Even if it were possible to keep the law in our actions, can we keep the law in our hearts?

   no

In His teaching ministry Jesus Christ amplified the law. He went beyond the written law to the spirit and meaning behind it. In so doing, He hammered home the message that if you want to be accepted by God based on your own merits, the standard is perfection both inwardly and outwardly.

The Law Stirs Up Sin

The sting of death is sin, and the power of sin is the law
(1 Corinthians 15:56).

1. According to this verse, what is the "sting of death"?   *sin*

2. What is the power of sin?   *law*

3. When a person is living under the law, what power will he be living under?

   power of sin

Since the law's standard is perfection and the power of sin is the law, is it any wonder that so many well-meaning Christians simply give up and say, "Christianity doesn't work"?

> *Since you died with Christ to the basic principles of this world, why, as though you still belonged to it, do you submit to its rules: "Do not handle! Do not taste! Do not touch!"? These are all destined to perish with use, because they are based on human commands and teachings. Such regulations indeed have an appearance of wisdom, with their self-imposed worship, their false humility and their harsh treatment of the body, but they lack any value in restraining sensual indulgence* (Colossians 2:20-23).

Explain

1. According to this passage, what have we died to? *basic principles of the world*

2. When you submit to the world's rules, what are you saying you belong to?
   world

3. As children of God, do we belong to the world? *no*

4. To whom do we belong? *Christ*

5. What are some of the rules that Paul mentions? *don't handle touch taste*

6. What do these rules have a false appearance of?
   righteousness

7. What are they based on? *human commands & teaching*

8. Do they have any value in restraining sensual indulgence? *Explain?*
   no

9. Then, does it make sense to submit to rules that do not work?

no

10. In Christ, we are totally loved, accepted, and forgiven, perfect in God's sight, and free of condemnation. In light of this, does it make sense for Christians to try to live up to the law when the law's sole purpose is to condemn men?

no

11. What would you conclude about the love of God if all you experienced as a Christian was condemnation?   no love

The law is a tough taskmaster. Its standard is perfection. It requires 100-percent obedience. The law has no mercy. If you stumble in just one point, you are guilty of breaking it all. On top of this, the very law that demands perfection is what stirs up sin in our lives. Living under the law is a no-win situation. There is no hope.

No wonder so many Christians experience fear, guilt, frustration, failure, and the inability to love God or others! When you are condemned by the law every day, your experience will be bleak. But don't fault the law. God's purpose for the law was and is so we could see our need for Christ. If you are experiencing guilt and condemnation through trying to keep the law, the law is doing its job.

9

The Real Problem of the Law

In the last several chapters, we have looked at verses that say the law condemns, it brings death, and it stirs up sin in our lives. After looking at these verses, it would be easy to conclude that the law is bad. As a matter of fact, after Paul stated the purpose of the law, people asked him if he was saying the law was sin (Romans 7:7). His response was an emphatic, "Certainly not!" The law was given by God. Therefore, it is holy, righteous, and good.

Think about the commands God gave to Moses: "Do not steal." "Do not murder." "Honor your father and mother." "Love the Lord your God." No one would say these commands are sin. Loving the Lord, honoring your father and mother, not stealing or murdering very beneficial to all. The problem is not with the commands. The problem is us.

Key Verse: Hebrews 8:7,8

For if there had been nothing wrong with that first covenant, no place would have been sought for another. But God found fault with the people and said: "The time is coming, declares the Lord, when I will make a new covenant with the house of Israel and with the house of Judah."

---

1. According to these verses, was there something wrong with the first covenant, the covenant God established with Israel at Mount Sinai?

2. If there had been nothing wrong with the first covenant, would there have been a need for a new covenant?

3. With whom did God find fault?

4. Did God say that He found fault with His covenant or with the law?

5. What, then, was the real problem of the first covenant?

6. Because God found fault with the people, what did He say He would do?

> *I do not understand what I do. For what I want to do I do not do, but what I hate I do. And if I do what I do not want to do, I agree that the law is good. As it is, it is no longer I myself who do it, but it is sin living in me. I know that nothing good lives in me, that is, in my flesh. For I have the desire to do what is good, but I cannot carry it out. For what I do is not the good I want to do; no, the evil I do not want to do— this I keep on doing. Now if I do what I do not want to do, it is no longer I who do it, but it is sin living in me that does it. So I find this law at work: When I want to do good, evil is right there with me. For in my inner being I delight in God's law; but I see another law at work in the members of my body, waging war against the law of my mind and making me a prisoner of the law of sin at work within my members. What a wretched man I am! Who will rescue me from this body of death?* (Romans 7:15-24).

1. In this passage, Paul is describing the experience of a man trying to live according to the law. When a person is living under the law, can he understand what he does?

2. Under the law, is a person able to do what he wants to do?

3. What does he end up doing?

4. Can you identify with the statement, "For what I want to do I do not do, but what I hate I do"?

5. Paul said, "It is no longer I myself who do it." What did he say was the source of his struggle?

6. What is the source of our struggle?

7. What did Paul know about his flesh?

8. Is the same true regarding your flesh?

9. Since nothing good lives in your flesh, even if you have the desire to do good, can you carry it out?

10. Even though you want to do good, what is it that you keep on doing?

11. Does this sound familiar?

12. Once again, what does Paul say is the source of us continuing to do the evil that we do not want to do?

13. What law did Paul find at work within him?

14. In his inner being, did Paul delight in God's law?

15. But what did he see at work in the members of his body?

16. As a result of the two laws waging war against each other, what did Paul become a prisoner of?

17. Go back and read through this passage. As you do, circle all the references to *I, me,* and *myself.* How many did you circle?

18. Under the law, who is our focus on?

19. Based on this, what would you say the real problem of trying to keep the law is?

20. Does man have the ability within him to free himself from the bondage, "What I want to do I do not do, but what I hate I do"?

21. In trying to live up to the law to gain God's acceptance, what conclusion did Paul come to about himself?

22. Has the law brought you to the same conclusion?

23. What was Paul's cry after coming to the conclusion, "Wretched man that I am"?

24. When we recognize our own wretchedness and our total inability to deliver ourselves from the bondage of sin, what should be our cry?

> *Thanks be to God—through Jesus Christ our Lord!* (Romans 7:25).

1. What was Paul's answer to his question, "Who will rescue me from this body of death?"

2. Who is the only One who can deliver us from the bondage of sin?

3. What, then, should be the answer to our cry, "Who will rescue me?"

> *Anyone who has died has been freed from sin* (Romans 6:7).

1. According to this verse, when is a person freed from sin?

2. Do you think this means dying physically or dying to our own self-efforts to keep the law?

> *For through the law I died to the law so that I might live for God. I have been crucified with Christ and I no longer live, but Christ lives in me. The life I live in the body, I live by faith in the Son of God, who loved me and gave himself for me* (Galatians 2:19,20).

1. What did Paul die to so he could live for God?

2. Since he had been crucified with Christ, what could Paul say about himself?

3. Who lives in Paul?

4. How does he live his life in the body?

5. Who was Paul's focus on, himself or Christ?

6. We have been crucified with Christ as well. What, then, is true of us?

7. Who is it that lives in us?

8. So, how should we live our lives in this body?

9. If we were still trying to keep the law, could we have faith in Christ to live His life through us?

10. If we were still trying to keep the law, who would our focus be on?

11. What did we say the real problem of trying to keep the law is?

12. Are you willing to get your eyes off the problem (yourself) and focus your attention on the solution (Jesus Christ)?

13. Are you willing to die to the law so you can live for God?

The real problem of the law is you and me. The law requires us to perform, to live up to its standards. But because sin dwells in our flesh, we are totally incapable of doing so. We cannot free ourselves from the power of sin. As a result, no matter how hard we try, or how strong our desire to do good is, we will always find ourselves saying, "What I want to do I do not do, but what I hate I do."

The solution to our struggle is to die to the law and come alive to the Lord Jesus Christ. You see, law and grace is more than an issue of how we live the Christian life. At the root of this issue is the *source* of the Christian life. Under the law, you and I are doing the living. Under grace, Christ lives. With us doing the living, there is no way to be free from the power of sin. Therefore, for us to be free, we must die to what keeps us under the power of sin—the law.

The Christian life is all Jesus and none of us. That is why it is so important for us to die to the law. As long as the law is active in our lives, we miss the experience of Christ living His life through us. He is the only One who can free us from the power of sin, and it is the grace of God that focuses our attention on Him.

10

You Cannot Mix Law and Grace

The most common problem that plagues Christianity today is the mixing of law and grace. It is the attitude that says, "God's grace gives us the ability to obey God's laws."

This is nothing new. The apostle Paul addressed the issue throughout his letters, primarily in the book of Galatians. As a matter of fact, the mixing of law and grace is commonly referred to as *Galatianism*. Jesus addressed this problem as well and illustrated the damage it causes by comparing it to pouring new wine into old wineskins.

Key Verse: Matthew 9:17

Neither do men pour new wine into old wineskins. If they do, the skins will burst, the wine will run out and the wineskins will be ruined. No, they pour new wine into new wineskins, and both are preserved.

---

1. Jesus uses the illustration of the wine and the wineskins to teach us a spiritual truth. Should new wine be poured into old wineskins?

2. What happens if new wine is poured into an old wineskin?

3. How are both the new wine and the old wineskin preserved?

4. Can new wine be contained in an old wineskin?

5. Let's apply this illustration to law and grace. Can the grace of God be contained within the context of the law?

6. What would happen if we tried to mix the two?

7. Can the purpose of the law and the purpose of grace be maintained if we mix the two?

8. How can we preserve the purpose of both law and grace?

> *You foolish Galatians! Who has bewitched you? Before your very eyes Jesus Christ was clearly portrayed as crucified. I would like to learn just one thing from you: Did you receive the Spirit by observing the law, or by believing what you heard? Are you so foolish? After beginning with the Spirit, are you now trying to attain your goal by human effort? Have you suffered so much for nothing—if it really was for nothing? Does God give you his Spirit and work miracles among you because you observe the law, or because you believe what you heard?* (Galatians 3:1-5).

1. How did Paul describe the believers in Galatia?

2. What did he say had happened to them?

3. What does it mean to be bewitched?

4. What did Paul portray clearly before the Galatians' eyes?

5. Whose efforts or work does Paul's portrayal indicate is important in our salvation—Christ's work on the cross or our obedience to the law?

6. What question did Paul ask the Galatians concerning how they received the Spirit?

7. What is the obvious answer?

8. How did you receive the Spirit of Christ—by observing the law or by believing what you heard?

9. What part did works of the law play in your receiving the Spirit?

10. Even though the Galatians knew they had received the Spirit by believing what they heard, how were they trying to attain their goal of living the Christian life?

11. Why is it foolish to think we can live the Christian life through our human efforts?

12. To hammer home his point, Paul asks the Galatians again, "Does God give you the Spirit and work miracles among you because you observe the law, or because you believe what you heard?" What is the obvious answer?

13. How does Paul's admonition to the Galatians apply to us today?

14. Why is it foolish to mix law and grace?

15. Can we experience the abundant life that Jesus promised by intermingling law and grace?

> *A little yeast works through the whole batch of dough* (Galatians 5:9).

1. *Yeast* is the word Jesus uses to describe the teaching of the Pharisees (see Matthew 16:6-12). They taught that you must obey the law to gain God's acceptance. How much of this teaching will spoil the entirety of grace?

> *I am astonished that you are so quickly deserting the one who called you by the grace of Christ and are turning to a different gospel— which is really no gospel at all. Evidently some people are throwing you into confusion and are trying to pervert the gospel of Christ. But even if we or an angel from heaven should preach a gospel other than the one we preached to you, let him be eternally condemned!* (Galatians 1:6-8)

1. What astonished Paul about the Galatians?

2. Who were they deserting?

3. How does Christ call us to Himself?

4. What did Paul say the Galatians were turning to?

5. What did he say about that gospel?

6. What was happening to the believers of Galatia due to erroneous teaching?

7. What happens to us when we try to mix law and grace?

8. What did Paul say these errant teachers were attempting to do?

9. What should happen to those who preach a gospel other than the one Paul preached?

10. Why do you think Paul felt so strongly about this doctrine of adding works of the law to the grace of Christ?

> *And if by grace, then it is no longer by works; if it were, grace would no longer be grace* (Romans 11:6).

1. According to this verse, are grace and works mutually exclusive?

2. If you try to combine law and grace, what happens to grace?

3. What value does grace have if we are trying to work for our salvation?

4. Are you intermingling law and grace in your life?

5. If so, does the Christian life seem confusing to you and impossible to live?

6. Do you realize that you are ruining the purpose of both the law and grace in your life?

The same grace that saves us is what sustains us in our Christian life. It only takes a little bit of the law, however, to ruin God's purpose in grace. You cannot mix the two. The new wine of grace cannot be contained in the old wineskin of the law.

C.I. Scofield writes in *Rightly Dividing the Word of Truth:*

> Law is God prohibiting and requiring; grace is God beseeching and bestowing. Law is a ministry of condemnation; grace, of forgiveness. Law curses; grace redeems from the curse. Law kills; grace makes alive. Law shuts every mouth before God; grace opens every mouth to praise Him. Law puts a great and guilty distance between man and God; grace makes guilty man nigh to God. Law says, "An eye for an eye, and a tooth for a tooth"; grace says, "Resist not evil; but whosoever shall smite thee on thy cheek, turn to him the other also." Law says, "Hate thine enemy"; grace says, "Love your enemies, bless them that despitefully use you." Law says, do and live; grace says, believe and live. Law never had a missionary; grace is to be preached to every creature. Law utterly condemns the best man; grace freely justifies the worst (Luke 23:43; Rom. 5:8; 1 Tim. 1:15; 1 Cor. 6:9-11). Law is a system of probation; grace, of favor. Law stones an adulteress; grace says, "Neither do I condemn thee: go, and sin no more." Under law the sheep dies for the shepherd: under grace the Shepherd dies for the sheep.
>
> Everywhere the Scriptures present law and grace in sharply contrasted spheres. The mingling of them in much of the current teaching of the day spoils both, for law is robbed of its terror, and grace of its freeness.

11

The Grace of God

As we have seen, life under the law is characterized by fear, guilt, failure, feelings of frustration and condemnation, and the inability to love God or others. It is a life where there is no peace or rest. It is the exact opposite of the abundant life Jesus promised: a life filled with love, joy, peace, patience, kindness, goodness, gentleness, and self-control.

Key Verse: Romans 5:1,2

Therefore, since we have been justified through faith, we have peace with God through our Lord Jesus Christ, through whom we have gained access by faith into this grace in which we now stand. And we rejoice in the hope of the glory of God.

1. Since we have been justified through faith, what do we now have with God?

2. What is it that we now stand in?

3. How did we gain access into this grace in which we now stand?

Grace Defined

We have spent a lot of time discussing the law and its ramifications in our lives, both as a lost person and as a saved person. But what about this grace in which we now stand? What is it? And what does it mean to live under the grace of God?

The grace of God is not something we can define with a simple phrase or sentence. We have made some feeble attempts, such as "God's unmerited favor," or the acrostic GRACE, God's Riches at Christ's Expense. But grace is so much bigger. Grace is the very nature of God. Trying to define grace is like trying to define God—a task too big for our finite minds.

We can see grace in action, however, through the person of Jesus Christ. John 1:14 tells us that Christ is full of grace and truth. When we look at Him and what He has done on our behalf, we can see what the grace of God is all about.

For you know the grace of our Lord Jesus Christ, that though he was rich, yet for your sakes he became poor, so that you through his poverty might become rich (2 Corinthians 8:9).

1. What did Paul say the Corinthians knew?

2. How did Jesus Christ express His grace to us?

3. Though He was rich, Jesus became poor for our sakes. Through His poverty, what do we become?

4. Is Paul referring to physical or spiritual riches?

5. From this verse, how would you define God's grace?

> *For it is by grace you have been saved, through faith—and this not from yourselves, it is the gift of God—not by works, so that no one can boast* (Ephesians 2:8,9).

1. According to these verses, how are we saved?

2. How does Paul describe this grace that saves us?

3. Can we work to earn God's grace?

4. Do we have anything to boast about? Why not?

> *But because of his great love for us, God, who is rich in mercy, made us alive with Christ even when we were dead in transgressions—it is by grace you have been saved* (Ephesians 2:4,5).

1. What did God do for us?

2. What was our condition when He did this?

3. What does a dead person need?

4. What was God's motivation for making us alive with Christ?

5. How does Paul say we have been saved?

6. We have been saved by grace. Specifically, how does this verse define being saved by grace?

> *In Him we have redemption through his blood, the forgiveness of sins, in accordance with the riches of God's grace that He lavished on us with all wisdom and understanding* (Ephesians 1:7,8).

1. According to this verse, where is redemption found?

2. Where is forgiveness found?

3. If you are "in Him," what do you have?

4. Our redemption and forgiveness are in accordance with what?

5. Redemption and forgiveness are part of the riches of God's grace. What does it mean that He "lavished these gifts on us"?

6. Did you and I need to be redeemed and forgiven?

7. Since you and I could not provide redemption and forgiveness for ourselves, could we say that we have them apart from the grace of God?

> *But when the kindness and love of God our Savior appeared, he saved us, not because of righteous things we had done, but because of his mercy. He saved us through the washing of rebirth and renewal by*

> *the Holy Spirit, whom he poured out on us generously through Jesus Christ our Savior, so that, having been justified by his grace, we might become heirs having the hope of eternal life* (Titus 3:4-7).

1. According to these verses, what appeared to mankind?

2. When the kindness and love of God our Savior appeared, what did God do?

3. Did He save us because of the righteous things we had done?

4. He saved us because of what?

5. How did He save us?

6. Through whom did all this take place?

7. According to this passage, how are we justified?

8. Having been justified, what do we become?

9. What is our hope?

Through these passages of Scripture, we have seen that it is God's grace that saves us, makes us alive together with Christ, redeems us, forgives us, justifies us, and gives us the hope of eternal life. All these passages show God reaching down through His Son Jesus Christ in love and mercy to do something for us that we could not do for ourselves. That is grace. It is a gift from God. We do not deserve it, nor could we earn it. And this is the grace of God in which we now stand.

> *With the help of Silas, whom I regard as a faithful brother, I have written to you briefly, encouraging you and testifying that this is the true grace of God. Stand fast in it* (1 Peter 5:12).

1. Why did Peter write this first letter?

2. What does Peter encourage us to do in the true grace of God?

3. What should our encouragement be to one another?

12

Freedom from Sin

The biggest criticism concerning the teaching of grace is that it will give people a license to sin. This criticism is nothing new. People asked the apostle Paul, "What then? Shall we sin because we are not under law but under grace?" (Romans 6:15). His answer was emphatic: "By no means!" God's grace does not lead us to a life of sin. God's grace is what frees us from the power of sin and enables us to experience the very life of Christ.

In the book of Philippians Paul tells us to work out our salvation with fear and trembling. Our salvation is the result of God's grace, and it is His grace that we are to work out. Yet God does not leave this task to our self-efforts. Paul goes on to say, "For it is God who works in you to will and to act according to his good purpose" (Philippians 2:13). Working out our salvation is not dependent on us. It is the result of God working in us. This is why we can stand confidently in the grace of God. God would never lead us to a life of sin. He will always lead us to will and act according to His good purpose. In light of this, let's take a closer look at how the grace of God is lived out in our day-to-day experience.

Key Verse: Galatians 2:20

I have been crucified with Christ and I no longer live, but Christ lives in me. The life I live in the body, I live by faith in the Son of God, who loved me and gave himself for me.

---

1. According to this verse, with whom have we been crucified?

2. Since we no longer live, who lives in us?

3. How are we to live our lives in our bodies?

4. Who is our faith to be in?

5. Why is Christ trustworthy?

6. Christ lives in us, and our role is to trust Him to live His life through us. Do you think He would lead us to a life of sin?

7. What kind of life do you think He desires to live through us?

> *You, however, are controlled not by the flesh but by the Spirit, if the Spirit of God lives in you. And if anyone does not have the Spirit of Christ, he does not belong to Christ* (Romans 8:9).

1. If the Spirit of God lives in you, who are you controlled by?

2. If the Spirit of God lives in you, are you controlled by the flesh?

3. Would you belong to Christ if the Spirit of God did not live in you?

4. Therefore, who is in control of every believer?

5. Would the Spirit of God lead us to a life of sin?

> *But if you are led by the Spirit, you are not under the law* (Galatians 5:18).

1. Who does this verse say we are led by?

2. If you are led by the Spirit, are you under the law?

3. As a believer, who, then, is in control of your life—the Spirit of God or the law?

We can stand confidently in the grace of God because Christ is the One who lives in us. It is His responsibility to live His life through us. We can be certain that the life He lives through us will be the life God desires for us. Let's take a closer look at what His life looks like.

> *For the grace of God that brings salvation has appeared to all men. It teaches us to say "No" to ungodliness and worldly passions, and to live self-controlled, upright and godly lives in this present age, while we wait for the blessed hope—the glorious appearing of our great God and Savior, Jesus Christ, who gave himself for us to redeem us from all wickedness and to purify for himself a people that are his very own, eager to do what is good* (Titus 2:11-14).

1. What does the grace of God bring to all men?

2. What does the grace of God teach us to do?

3. God's grace teaches us to say "No" to ungodliness and worldly passions, and it doesn't stop with just teaching us to say no. What kind of life does it teach us to live?

4. What did Jesus Christ redeem us from?

5. What are God's very own people eager to do?

6. Why are they eager to do what is good?

7. According to this verse, does the grace of God give a person a license to sin?

> *So I say, live by the Spirit, and you will not gratify the desires of the flesh. For the flesh desires what is contrary to the Spirit, and the Spirit what is contrary to the flesh. They are in conflict with each other, so that you do not do what you want* (Galatians 5:16,17).

1. How do these verses say we should live?

2. What is the result of living by the Spirit?

3. Do these verses say anything about cleaning up the flesh in order to live by the Spirit?

4. Are the flesh and the Spirit in conflict with each other?

5. Do they have the same desires?

6. Therefore, is the Spirit ever going to lead us to fulfill the desires of the flesh?

> *But he said to me, "My grace is sufficient for you, for my power is made perfect in weakness." Therefore I will boast all the more gladly about my weakness, so that Christ's power may rest on me* (2 Corinthians 12:9).

1. What did God tell Paul was sufficient for him?

2. Do we have the power to say no to sin in and of ourselves?

3. Whose power do we need?

4. When is God's power made perfect?

5. In our weakness, who do we have to depend on to live the Christian life?

6. Can you see why Paul boasted about his weaknesses?

7. If Christ's power rests on us in our weaknesses, what does this say about your self-efforts?

8. Have you learned that God's grace is sufficient?

9. God says we can be free from the power of sin. This freedom comes from resting in the grace of God. Are you willing to die to your self-efforts and come alive to the grace of God and go free?

13

Living
by a Higher Law

Thus far, we have learned that the grace of God teaches us to say no to ungodliness and wordly passions and to live self-contolled, upright, and godly lives. We have also learned that as children of God we are led by the Spirit of God and not the law. And certainly, we can be confident that the Spirit of God is not going to lead us into a life of sin. From God's vantage point, however, saying no to sin and living upright lives is not His *complete* purpose for our lives. He desires for us to live by a higher law. It is called the law of love.

Key Verse: Galatians 5:13,14

You, my brothers, were called to be free. But do not use your freedom to indulge the flesh; rather, serve one another in love. The entire law is summed up in a single command: "Love your neighbor as yourself."

1. What were we called to be?

2. Can we use this freedom to indulge the flesh?

3. Rather, how are we to use our freedom?

4. How does Paul sum up the law?

> *Do not get drunk on wine, which leads to debauchery. Instead, be filled with the Spirit* (Ephesians 5:18).

1. What does this verse say we are not to do?

2. When you are drunk on wine, what controls you?

3. What does this lead to?

4. Instead, what are we to be controlled by?

5. Therefore, who are we to be controlled by?

6. What does it mean to be "filled with the Spirit"? Many of us have asked that question out of total frustration. We know what the words say, but exactly how do we go about being filled with the Spirit? Ephesians 3 provides a practical answer.

> *I pray that out of his glorious riches he may strengthen you with power through his Spirit in your inner being, so that Christ may dwell in your hearts through faith. And I pray that you, being rooted and established in love, may have power, together with all the saints, to grasp how wide and long and high and deep is the love of Christ, and to*

know this love that surpasses knowledge—that you may be filled to the
measure of all the fullness of God (Ephesians 3:16-19).

1. This is Paul's prayer for all Christians. What does he ask God to do in our lives?

2. How does God strengthen us with power?

3. Where does this strengthening take place?

4. What is this power is for?

5. What is the result of knowing the love of Christ that "surpasses knowledge"?

6. If you are filled to the measure of all the fullness of God, what are you filled with?

7. If you are filled with the knowledge of God's love and grace, what controls you?

8. Can you be "filled to the measure of the fullness of God" and not be filled with the Spirit?

9. So what does "being filled with the Spirit" mean?

10. Being filled with the Spirit means that you are filled and controlled by the love and grace of God. How is being filled by the love and grace of God going to affect how you treat others?

> *Be kind and compassionate to one another, forgiving each other, just as in Christ God forgave you* (Ephesians 4:32).

1. How are we to forgive others?

> *Accept one another, then, just as Christ accepted you, in order to bring praise to God* (Romans 15:7).

1. How are we to accept one another?

> *My command is this: Love each other as I have loved you* (John 15:12).

1. How are we to love others?

2. Could we forgive, accept, and love others apart from knowing Christ has forgiven, accepted, and loved us?

3. Would we be able to know Christ has forgiven, accepted, and loved us apart from being filled with the Spirit of God?

> *But the fruit of the Spirit is love, joy, peace, patience, kindness, goodness, faithfulness, gentleness and self-control. Against such things there is no law* (Galatians 5:22,23)

1. When we are controlled by the Spirit of God, what is being produced in our lives?

2. Is there a law against such things as love, patience, kindness, goodness, faithfulness, gentleness and self-control?

> *All over the world this gospel is bearing fruit and growing, just as it has been doing among you since the day you heard it and understood God's grace in all its truth* (Colossians 1:6).

1. According to this verse, what does the gospel produce?

2. When does a person start bearing fruit?

3. What must we understand about the gospel in order to bear fruit?

4. Would this fruit be different from the fruit of the Spirit?

5. So, if we are going to experience love, joy, peace, patience, kindness, goodness, faithfulness, and self-control, what must we understand?

6. As we are filled with the Spirit, what is the Spirit of God going to lead us to a deeper understanding of?

> *But grow in the grace and knowledge of our Lord and Savior Jesus Christ* (2 Peter 3:18).

1. What is Peter's encouragement to us?

2. When we grow in the grace and knowledge of our Lord Jesus Christ, what are we growing in?

3. What are we going to pass on to others as we grow in the grace of God?

4. In your own words, state the importance of knowing the difference between law and grace.

Jesus Christ said, "All men will know that you are my disciples, if you love one another" (John 13:35). There is only one way that will happen, and it is not through obedience to the law. We must first receive God's love and grace, or we will have nothing to give. But if we will receive God's love and become channels of that love to others, we can walk in the assurance that we are fulfilling the highest purpose of God in our daily lives, and that purpose is: "A new command I give you: Love one another. As I have loved you, so you must love one another" (John 13:34).